Unsolved Murders

A Stunning Look At the Worlds Most Famous Unsolved Murder Cases, Unsolved Mysteries, Unsolved Crimes And What Really Happened

Table of Contents

Do you want more books?

How would you like books arriving in your inbox each week?

Don't worry they are FREE!

We publish books on all sorts of non-fiction niches and send them out to our subscribers each week to spread the love.

All you have to do is sign up and you're good to go!

Just go to the link at the end of this book, sign up, sit back and wait for your book downloads to arrive!

We couldn't have made it any easier! Enjoy!

Introduction

I want to thank you and congratulate you for purchasing the book, "Unsolved Murders: *A Stunning Look At the Worlds Most Famous Unsolved Murder Cases, Unsolved Mysteries, Unsolved Crimes And What Really Happened*".

It would not be wrong to assume that at one point of time, all of us would have considered taking up a job at the FBI or CIA mainly because of our obsession with solving crimes.

There have been times when we would have wondered why we are obsessed with crime solving so much. We owe it to the many detective novels we grew up reading, the many TV shows that have been made over the years with the central theme of crime solving and the many brilliant movies that have graced our screens.

The habit of analyzing things and arriving at a conclusion was inculcated in us first when we were young through these books, shows and movies. Man is inquisitive by nature and this instinct has only grown stronger over the years by these external influences. It wouldn't come as a surprise if most of you had tried playing the detective when your neighbor's cat went missing or when you see someone new in the neighborhood.

But how often have we reached a dead end during one of our sleuth games? When we read a mystery puzzle somewhere, we wouldn't rest until we know the answer. Sometimes, no answers can be found no matter how hard one tries. This is precisely what this book is all about.

We bring to you sixteen deadly and unsolved murder cases that shook the world once upon a time. Even though this will prove to be an interesting read, our heart goes out to the families of these victims who haven't had closure in years. Each case is different from the others yet they are all united by a single fact- they are all unsolved!

Having said that, are you ready to leaf through the next few blood stained pages? If yes, help yourselves to some of the intriguing cases handpicked by us for the inquisitive you! Don't try to solve them though. Well, they have remained unsolved over the years for a reason.

Tread carefully for the path is filled with blood and gore! Read at your own risk.

Case 1:
The abduction and murder of Amber Hagerman

Tentative time: January 13- 17, 1996

Place: Arlington, Texas

Amber Rene Hagerman was a nine year old kid hailing from Texas who was abducted and killed.

It all began when Amber went out to ride her bike with her brother Ricky. They were initially circling their grandparents' block. Slowly they went past the allowed perimeter to ride their bikes on a ramp on the parking lot near an empty grocery store. Children often used to ride their bikes on that ramp and it was only natural that Amber wanted to play there with her brother.

As time progressed, Ricky was worried that their mother would scold them for riding out so far and decided to get back home. However Amber was not satisfied. She wanted to go for one last ride on the ramp and stayed back.

When Ricky got back home, the family was concerned about leaving Amber alone at the ramp and sent him back to fetch her. However, when Ricky came back to the ramp, Amber was nowhere to be seen. Amber and Ricky's grandfather, Jimmie Whitson, scoured the area in his truck but could not find Amber anywhere.

When Jimmie reached the parking lot where the ramp was, the police were already there investigating the scene. The police had been called in by a man who lived nearby who had heard screaming and had seen another man carrying a little girl to his pickup truck. However, the only thing that was still left in the parking lot when the police came was Amber's bike.

In the next few days, Amber's family pleaded for her safe return by appearing on television. However, the family was in for a massive blow when they discovered the naked body of Amber lying on a creek bed near an apartment complex. Amber was killed by slitting her throat.

Since there was no other witness, except the man who had called 911, and not much evidence was present on the scene of crime, the Police had nothing to take this case forward. This case remains unsolved till this day.

Why is this case an important one for us to know? Well, this abduction and murder paved the way for the Amber alert systems, named after Amber Hagerman.

Case 2:
The murder of Betsy Aardsma

Tentative time: November 28, 1969

Place: Pennsylvania

Betsy Aardsma was 22 years old when she was murdered. She was an English major who hailed from Michigan. She was attending the Pennsylvania State University.

On the day of the murder, Betsy was doing research in the university library for one of her papers.

Someone had stabbed Betsy once through the heart at around 4:55 p.m. Two men were seen running out of the library a minute after the stabbing. Before running out, they had called out to the desk clerk asking them to help out Betsy.

Since Betsy was wearing a red colored top at the time of the murder, the impact of the stabbing was not known to the people who were trying to help her out. The people at the library had assumed that Betsy had fallen unconscious from a seizure attack and tried giving her a CPR to resuscitate her. Only during the physical examination at the hospital, was the severity of the stab discovered.

The two men who ran out of the library remain unidentified till this day. The Pennsylvania State Police is still on the process of finding the murderers, even after forty five years.

Case 3:
The Black Dahlia

Tentative time: January, 1947

Place: Los Angeles

Elizabeth Short, who was born in 1924, was given the nickname "the black Dahlia". This murder case is one of the most popular unsolved cases till date purely because of the gruesome manner in which the murder was committed. Books and movies have been made around this case. Nevertheless, it remains unsolved.

Elizabeth Short was discovered dead on January 15, 1947 in the Leimert Park in Los Angeles. Her body was sliced into half by a deep cut on the waist. When the police discovered Short's body, it was completely nude and drained of blood.

Apart from that, the corners of her mouth were slashed into deep cuts up to her ears. What was more gruesome than these cuts was the way her nude body was positioned by the murderer. Her hands were held above her head with the elbows bent at right angles.

The cause of death was zeroed down to severe blood loss as a result of the multiple cuts and the shock as a result of concussion she suffered from the blow to her head.

The Police were successful in identifying many suspects. However, no one has been convicted yet. If you thought the case ended here, then you are wrong. The murderer obviously wanted this murder case to hog the limelight for a long time. Every time he felt the media was giving less importance to the case, he contacted the newspapers.

During one such instance, an envelope consisting of the personal belongings of Short along with a small address book carrying the name of "Mark Hensen" was also mailed. Interestingly, Mark Hensen was the last person to have seen Elizabeth Short alive. However, he was found innocent.

Because of the wide media coverage and the hype surrounding the case, many people over the years have claimed to be involved in this case just to become famous. However, the hunt for the murderer continues still, even after 68 years.

Case 4:
The murder of Bob Cane

Tentative time: June 29, 1978

Place: Scottsdale, Arizona

Bob Cane was a well-known sitcom artist. His role as "Colonel Robert E. Hogan" in the sitcom called the "Hogan's Heroes" was well received and appreciated. But what made him more popular than his roles was the mystery surrounding his death.

Crane was residing at his Winfield Place Apartments in Scottsdale, Arizona. At this point of time, he was busy acting in his play "Beginner's Luck" which was being played at the nearby Windmill Dinner Theatre. It was his co-star, Victoria Ann Berry who discovered his body in his apartment.

Originally, Crane and Berry were supposed to meet for lunch. Since Crane did not turn up, Berry went to his apartment in search of him only to discover his dead body.

When the body was discovered, an electric cord was secured tight around his neck and the cause of death was ascertained as bludgeoning even though no weapon was found in the scene. It was speculated from the bludgeoning marks that a camera tripod might have been the weapon used by the murderer.

At this point, a wave of suspicion rose against Crane's friend, John Henry Carpenter. Due to lack of evidence, the police were unable to press charges against Carpenter. Apparently, Carpenter had called Crane's apartment many times on the day of the murder. When Carpenter actually turned up at

Crane's house, he did not show any signs of surprise on seeing the police there.

When Carpenter's car was searched, they found blood stains on the seats. Preliminary blood tests proved that the blood matched Crane's blood group. Since DNA testing was not discovered until later, the police were unable to determine if it was indeed Crane's blood. The case hit a deadlock at this juncture.

The case hit the surface when it was reopened in 1990 by the Maricopa County. With the introduction of DNA testing, the police were able to conduct the requisite tests on the blood samples taken from Carpenter's car.

However the test did not yield positive results for the police to press charges against Carpenter. However, fresh evidence was brought forward by a detective handling the case. He was able to get his hands on a picture of the car in which he discovered what was believed to be brain tissue on the insides of the car.

Based on this evidence, Carpenter was arrested and charged for the murder of Bob Crane. However, Carpenter was found innocent during the trial. With the innocence of Carpenter becoming evident, the Police had no more leads to take the case forward.

With the case hitting a dead end, the murderer of Bob Crane is yet to be found and convicted.

Case 5:
The murder of the Grimes sisters

Tentative time: December 28, 1956 – January 22, 1957

Place: Chicago

Would you be thrilled to know that Elvis Presley was also a part of this case?

Patricia and Barbara Grimes were sisters who hailed from Chicago. They were 13 years and 15 years old respectively when they disappeared. On December 28, 1956, the sisters had gone out to watch 'Love Me Tender', an Elvis Presley movie. There were people who saw the girls standing in line for popcorn at around 9:30 p.m.

Despite the movie finishing by 11 p.m., the girls did not return home. After waiting till 2:15 a.m., their mother had called the police. This culminated in one of the biggest missing persons hunt in the state of Chicago. At one point of time, Elvis Presley issued a statement itself, realizing the gravity of the situation, asking the girls to go home safely.

All the efforts to rescue the girls hit a dead end when their naked bodies were found on January 22, 1957. Leonard Prescott, a construction worker, found the bodies of the girls next to German Church Road. Medical examinations proved that Barbara went through molestation before she was killed.

Unlike the other cases, this case had many suspects but further investigations yielded no fruitful results.

Case 6:
The murder of Julia Wallace

Tentative time: January, 1931

Place: Liverpool, England

Julia Wallace was found murdered on January 20, 1931. Even though Julia's husband, William Herbert Wallace was convicted for the murder of his wife, he was later found innocent by the Court of Criminal Appeal.

The sequences of events that make the case more intriguing are as follows. William was playing a game at the Liverpool Chess club, the night before the murder of Julia. During the course of the game, a message was handed over to William. The message was passed over a telephone call before William arrived at the Chess club.

According to the message, William was expected to arrive at 25, Menlove Gardens East, Liverpool at 7:30 p.m. on January 20. The supposed intention of this meeting was to discuss insurance with R.M. Qualtrough.

William followed the instructions and tried reaching the destination. To his dismay, there was no address such as 25, Menlove Gardens East. He spent a considerable amount of time trying to find out the address. He was seen inquiring a patrolling police officer and a newsagent to help him locate the address, but of no use.

After searching for forty five minutes, William returned home. As William was trying to enter his home, he met his neighbors who were going out and told them about his problems in entering the home. Finally, when William entered the home through the back door, he found his wife beaten to death in the living room of the house. William was arrested for the murder of Julia two weeks after her death.

What makes this case special was that this was the first case in the history of British legal system, where an appeal was granted in a case after the completion of re-examination. It was also observed as an unbeatable case in the British legal history. And the crime remains unsolved till this day as there was not much evidence on the scene to proceed further.

Case 7:
The Axeman of New Orleans

Tentative time: May, 1918 to October, 1919

Place: New Orleans, Louisiana

As the name suggests, the Axeman killed his victims with an axe. In some of the crime scenes, the axe was also used to break open the front door. What made the Axeman more notorious was the way he chose his victims.

There was no pattern whatsoever thereby making it difficult for the Police to profile him and anticipate his next moves. His victims were chosen at random, ranging from a pregnant woman to an infant. This unpredictable nature of the Axeman made him different from the other serial killers.

When it comes to serial killers, there is always a said pattern in the murders which makes it easy to profile them and understand their motives behind the murders thereby making it easy to track their next victims. In this case though, the lack of a pattern left everyone in the dark rendering them unable to do nothing but wait for fresh evidence to turn up at the next crime scene. This precisely made the Axeman one of the most dangerous serial killers in the beginning of the twentieth century.

He taunted the entire city with his killings. The Axeman went on to call himself as a demon from hell in many of his letters to the newspapers.

It was evident from his letters that he enjoyed the power he was wielding and the fear he was spreading. In one of his letters, he went on to reveal the timing of his next murder. He stated that he would kill exactly at fifteen minutes after midnight on March 19, 1919.

However, he also mentioned that he would not attack the regions where jazz music was being played. Jazz music was played across the entire city to ward off the Axeman. No murders were committed that night.

The number of victims of the Axeman amounted to 12 as of October, 1919. Without a profile, it was becoming a herculean task to identify the actual murderer. There were many speculations as to who the Axeman would be. However without much evidence in hand to pin anyone for these murders, the speculations soon died.

There was also a rumour that the Axeman was one Joseph Momfre who suffered death in the hands of a widow of one of his victims. However that story too died with the passage of time. He stopped killing by October, 1919 and that was the last anyone ever heard from him.

Case 8:
The murder of the "Beautiful Cigar girl"

Tentative time: July, 1841

Place: Hoboken, New Jersey

Mary Rogers, born in 1820, was commonly called as the "Beautiful Cigar girl". She was working in a New York City based tobacco shop. The establishment was owned by John Anderson. Since Mary's beauty lured in more customers, Anderson saw no harm in paying her well for the job. Mary was well liked by all the customers. She was also known for casting flirtatious glances at some of the good looking customers.

On October 5th, 1838, Mary's mother, Phoebe Rogers had contacted the New York Sun with the news that her daughter had gone missing. She even divulged the contents of the suicide note supposedly left behind by Mary Rogers.

However, the very next day, Mary's disappearance was explained by the Times and Commercial Intelligence newspaper. According to the newspaper, Mary had gone to Brooklyn for a day to visit her friend. It was later discovered that the whole disappearance act was a publicity stunt staged by John Anderson to attract more customers to his shop.

Well, the staged act turned into a reality three years later. The last person to hear from Mary Rogers was her fiancé, Daniel Payne. She had contacted him on 25th July, 1841 and informed him about her trip to visit her family.

However, she did not visit her family as planned. Instead, her body was found in the Hudson River, Hoboken. Since she was well liked by everyone, her death caused a lot of stir and increased the tension surrounding her death.

It was believed initially that she died because of a faulty abortion procedure performed by abortionist, Madame Restell. It was also speculated that it was Madame Restell who dumped her body in the Hudson River. However, there was not much evidence to press charges against Madame Restell even though a woman named Frederica Loss vouched that Mary's untimely death was due to the faulty abortion procedure performed by Madame Restell.

On the other hand, there was another speculation doing the rounds that Mary Rogers was a victim of gang violence. However, the case was nowhere close to being solved. Amidst all this hype and press coverage, Daniel Payne killed himself by consuming poison. This just added on to the confusion surrounding the case.

Though unsolved, it was a famous case back then which even prompted to Edgar Allan Poe to fictionalize Mary Rogers in his work "The Mystery of Marie Roget".

Case 9:
The boy in the box

Tentative time: February, 1957

Place: Philadelphia, Pennsylvania

The victim of this case is unidentified till date. However, it was a boy belonging to the age group 4 to 6 years when he was murdered.

The boy was murdered and stuffed inside a cardboard box. His body was wrapped in a plaid blanket. The box was left lying in the Fox chase section of Philadelphia. The boy was first discovered by a muskrat trapper who was checking his traps in that area. However, he did not report this to the police. The box was discovered again by a college student who went into the area chasing a rabbit.

However, he was too scared to report it immediately. He finally mustered the courage to call the police only the next day.

The boy's face was plastered across all newspapers and his photographs made the rounds in different media. But nobody came forward claiming the boy. As a result of which, the police were unable to identify the suspects and press charges.

However the anonymity of the boy did not deter the speculators. Two prominent theories came up during the investigation. The first one suggested that the boy belonged to a foster home located in that region. He was a victim of domestic violence.

This theory was discarded once the police discovered that the person running the foster home was innocent. The second theory suggested that the boy was sold to an abusive family by his parents for money and that the boy was murdered by the members of the abusive family. However, this theory was not taken seriously either because the accuser was suffering from severe mental illness.

Various blood tests and DNA tests did not yield any fruitful results and the identity of the boy is a mystery this day. Without an identity, there is nothing substantial for the police to take the case forward.

Case 10:
The murder of Thelma Todd

Tentative time: December, 1935

Place: Roosevelt Highway

Thelma Todd, also known as "Hot Toddy" was a famous American actress during the late 1920s and early 1930s. At this point of time, she was living in an apartment above the café she owned on the Roosevelt Highway. The café was called the Sidewalk café. She also had a garage in proximity to the café.

Thelma was discovered dead inside her car in the garage on December 15, 1935. Because Thelma came across as a depressed person most of the time, the first bet about her untimely death was that she committed suicide. But further probing into the crime scene proved otherwise. There were traces of blood in Thelma's mouth and there were blood stains inside the car as well.

An intriguing piece of evidence was a smudged hand print that was discovered on the car door. Since the garage was situated uphill, it would not have been possible for Thelma to climb the three hundred odd steps with her high blood pressure levels while wearing high heels.

Since many people had heard of Thelma speaking about suicide, her death was labelled as suicide when her case was brought to trial. However no explanation was offered in connection with the blood stains or the hand print. There was no match found when the hand print was put to test. These questions remain unanswered till this day.

Case 11:
The murder of Rashawn Brazell

Tentative time: February, 2004

Place: Brooklyn

This is considered as one of the most horrific murder cases in the history of New York State. Rashawn Brazell was 19 years old when he was murdered.

It all began on the morning of February 14, 2005. Rashawn was supposed to meet his accountant that morning and meet his mother for lunch. However his plans did not materialize when a stranger rang the bell of his house.

The two of them, after a brief conversation, headed out to the Gates Avenue Station together. Later, the two were seen exiting the subway at Nostrand Avenue station in Bedford, Stuyvesant, according to the accounts of several eye witnesses. That was the last anyone ever saw Rashawn alive.

Two bags containing body parts were found at the subway station four days after Rashawn was reported missing. The fingerprints of the victim were found to match with that of Rashawn. This makes it the one of the most gruesome murder cases in the history of America.

The police were unable to recover any information in connection with the stranger who had accompanied Rashawn. His identity remains a mystery till this day. Over the years, no new leads cropped up to assist the police in solving this murder. This gruesome murderer is still out on the loose.

Case 12:
The murder of Suzanne Jovin

Tentative time: 1998

Place: College Street

Suzanne Jovin was a senior student at Yale University. She was 21 years old at the time of her murder. She was a German born American. She had volunteered as a tutor and was a part of the university chorus. She worked in the Davenport dining hall during her free time.

On the night of her murder, Jovin decided to return the keys of the car she had borrowed and walked towards the Yale police communications centre. She ran into a classmate, Peter Stein, on her way at around 9:22 p.m.

According to the statement given by Stein, Jovin had no plans for the evening and intended to get back home after returning the keys and turn in early as she was feeling tired. Jovin was holding a piece of paper in her hand, according to Stein. He also added that she was looking perfectly calm and serene.

Apparently, after her brief encounter with Stein, Jovin had walked to the communications centre and returned the keys. She was last seen by the people at the communications centre between 9:25 p.m. and 9:30 p.m. She was last seen walking on the road north-east of the College Street.

A call was made to 911 at around 9:55 p.m. by an anonymous person who reported seeing a woman bleeding at 2 miles from the College street, precisely where Jovin was seen last.

When the police arrived at the scene four minutes after the call, they found Jovin bleeding profusely on the road. She had been stabbed seventeen times in the back of the neck and the head. Her throat was also found to be slit. She was rushed to the Yale New Haven hospital where she was pronounced dead at around 10:26 p.m.

Medical examination resulted in the extraction of the DNA from under the fingernails of Jovin. Apart from this, the forensic team had discovered Jovin's fingerprints and a partial print of another person on the soda bottle that was lying at the crime scene.

There were also accounts of a brown van being spotted near the crime scene and a man running in the direction opposite to that of the spot where Jovin's body was found.

What made the case more mysterious was the mail sent by Jovin before her death. She had mentioned a mysterious someone in her last mail. The police could neither find a match for the partial fingerprint nor trace this someone Jovin had mentioned in the mail.

Even though there were speculations of Jovin's thesis advisor being guilty, he was proved to be innocent as the days went by. With the evidence pointing in no particular direction, the police could not identify the murderer and convict him. The identity of the murderer is a mystery till this day.

Case 13:
Oscar Romero

Tentative time: March 24, 1980

Place: El Salvador

Oscar Romero was born in August, 1917 and was named Óscar Arnulfo Romero Galdámez. He was the fourth archbishop of San Salvador. Romero was assassinated on March 24, 1980 when he was conducting a mass at the hospital La Divina Providencia.

A sermon immediately followed his assassination. This was the sermon Romero had given the day before his death. In his last sermon, he had addressed the soldiers of El Savador asking them to refrain from repressing citizens and depriving them of their basic rights. He also asked the soldiers to act as men of God and follow the path shown by God.

The madness did not end here. At the funeral of Romero, a smoke grenade was activated. Numerous shots were fired which ended up killing around fifty people and wounding many others who had come for the funeral. The gunfire continued until Romero's body was laid down.

It was later discovered that the assassination of Romero was funded by the United States and the assassination was lead by a former Major, Roberto D'Aubuisson. Alvaro Rafael Saravia, an active member of the assassination squad was charged in 2004 for assisting, conspiring and participating in the assassination and was asked to pay a fine of ten million dollars.

Even though, Saravia was made liable for being a part of the assassination plan, there was not much evidence to link him as the murderer or to the killings that happened at the funeral of Romero. The murderer of Romero and the number of people who died at his funeral remain unnamed till this day.

Case 14:
The Zodiac Killer

Tentative time: December, 1968 to October, 1969

Place: Benicia, Vallejo, Lake Berryessa and San Francisco

The Zodiac killer turned out to be one of the second most notorious serial killers after Jack the Ripper. He was charged for the murder of five people between December, 1968 and October, 1969. However, the Zodiac killer claimed to have killed 37 people.

His victims ranged between the age group 16 and 29. His other victims were unidentified due to lack of evidence to connect them with the Zodiac killer. No other case would have had as many suspects as this case. There were more than 2500 suspects. However none of them were found guilty.

Poor forensic technology prevalent at that point of time made it impossible to ascertain who the murderer was. Apart from the pleasure he derived from the murders, the Zodiac killer amused himself by taunting the local authorities.

He sent many letters to the local newspapers that were cryptic in nature. It was precisely this reason that earned him the nickname, the Zodiac killer. The identity of the Zodiac killer is still a question till this day. Lack of evidence was the sole reason behind which the Zodiac killer managed to escape from the shackles of law.

Case 15:
Jack the Ripper

Tentative time: 1888

Place: White chapel district, London

You already should have guessed that Jack the Ripper would definitely feature in this book!

Jack the Ripper is perhaps the most notorious serial killer known to date. Like all serial killers, he had a way of choosing his victims and dealing with them. He terrorized the district of White chapel with his killings. His victims were female prostitutes and they were all killed in the same fashion.

Their throats were slit and their abdomens were mutilated completely. He also removed specific organs from his victims but the reason for the same could not be known. Because of this particular mode of killing his victims, he was suspected to be either a doctor or a butcher as knowledge about anatomy is essential when it comes to extracting organs in such a fashion.

His five well known victims were Elizabeth Stride, Mary Ann Nichols, Annie Chapman, Mary Jane Kelly and Catherine Eddowes. There was no dearth for speculations as to who Jack the Ripper might be.

Despite the killings following a said pattern, it was not possible to trace them back to a single person and convict them. Nobody has been charged for these murders till date. Jack the Ripper is in fact one of the most elusive serial killers that history has ever seen.

Case 16:
Jack the Stripper

Tentative time: 1964- 1965

Place: London

No, we have not misspelt the name of Jack the Ripper. Jack the Stripper was a different serial killer and had his style of killing people. His killings were collectively known as the Hammersmith murders or the London nudes cases or the Hammersmith nudes cases.

Just like Jack the Ripper, he targeted only female prostitutes. He is believed to have murdered around eight prostitutes between 1964 and 1965. After killing his victims, he dumped their bodies in the Thames River. The only evidence that could be garnered by the police from all these murders was traces of paint that were found on the bodies of all the victims.

Based on this solitary piece of evidence, Mungo Ireland was zeroed in as a suspect. Ireland was working as a security guard in the factory where the paint was being manufactured. However, the case did not progress any further with Ireland committing suicide. Carbon monoxide poisoning was determined as the cause of death.

The interesting part that made Ireland a strong suspect was his suicide note addressed to his wife. He had stated that he could not stick it in any longer and explicitly mentioned that "To save you and the police looking for me, I'll be in the garage."

Even though his suicide note might have confirmed his involvement in the murders, evidences later proved that

Ireland was not in town when one of the murders was committed. This piece of information was sufficient to prove that Mungo Ireland was not Jack the Stripper.

Even though many other suspects were identified, there was not enough evidence to press charges against any of them and convict them.

Conclusion

That brings us to the end of this mysterious journey into the past! We hope that you do not lose your beauty sleep over these cases. Most of these cases were not solved at the time of committing of the crime because of the lack of advanced technology and medical facilities to process the evidence and trace the murderer.

By the time necessary advancements in the field of medicine and technology were in place, it was too late to start from scratch. Nevertheless these cases have been quite a nightmare to not only the families of the victims but also to the police.

We hope you found it an intriguing read!

Thank you and good luck!

Do you want more books?

How would you like books arriving in your inbox each week?

They're FREE!

We publish books on all sorts of non-fiction niches and send them to our subscribers each week to spread the love.

All you have to do is sign up and you're good to go!

Just go to the link below, sign up, sit back and wait for your book downloads to arrive.

We couldn't have made it any easier. Enjoy!

www.LibraryBugs.com

www.ingramcontent.com/pod-product-compliance
Lightning Source LLC
Chambersburg PA
CBHW030551290526
45786CB00004B/1961